A Guy's Guide to Sexuality and Sexual Identity in the 21st Century

A YOUNG MAN'S GUIDE
TO CONTEMPORARY ISSUES™

A Guy's Guide to Sexuality and Sexual Identity in the 21st Century

Joe Craig

ROSEN
PUBLISHING®

New York

Published in 2012 by The Rosen Publishing Group, Inc.
29 East 21st Street, New York, NY 10010

Library of Congress Cataloging-in-Publication Data

Craig, Joe, 1960–
A guy's guide to sexuality and sexual identity in the 21st century/
Joe Craig. — 1st ed.
  p. cm. — (A young man's guide to contemporary issues)
Includes bibliographical references and index.
ISBN 978-1-4488-5524-7 (library binding)
1. Masculinity—Juvenile literature. 2. Sex—Juvenile literature. 3.
Gender identity—Juvenile literature. I. Title.
BF692.5.C73 2012
155.3'32–dc23
                                                    2011018766

Manufactured in the United States of America

CPSIA Compliance Information: Batch #W12YA: For further information, contact Rosen Publishing, New York,
New York, at 1-800-237-9932.

Contents

INTRODUCTION

We want to be men, not boys. Every day, we behave in ways that we think "real men" act in order to prove our manhood to others—and to ourselves. And this constant effort isn't easy. From a very young age, we're conditioned to believe that we must prove our masculinity to others in order to become men.

Your sense of your own masculinity can often be bound up with your sexuality, or the way you express your

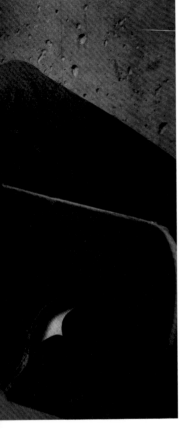

Guys are expected to horse around with each other, but close friends can also be affectionate, sensitive, and mutually supportive.

awareness of your biological sex. This book explores sexuality and how it affects our daily lives. First, we'll investigate some common stereotypes about men and women and how they should look, act, and speak. These stereotypes are found everywhere we turn, particularly in the images and messages constantly streaming from the mass media. They're false truths, but they still affect how we identify ourselves and interact with others.

As a result of these relentless messages of gender stereotypes, we're conditioned to believe that boys and girls are naturally and inherently different, not just physically but also emotionally, intellectually, and in terms of behavior. This inherent difference between the sexes is not in fact true. But belief in essential differences between the sexes is one of the most important determining factors for how we view ourselves, how others view us, and how we craft our identities.

Different boys have different experiences depending on their sexual identity. One's sexual identity is how one identifies his sexuality to himself and to others—as homosexual, bisexual, or heterosexual. Sexual identity is connected to, but not the same thing as, sexual orientation, which describes a person's sexual attractions to women, men, both, or neither. Sexual orientation is what we feel inside, but sexual identity is the image and attitudes we present to other people. This book will examine different sexual identities and orientations and the ways in which they coincide or conflict with social norms and traditional gender expectations.

Finally, this book will examine how sexuality, sexual identity, and sexual orientation play out in daily life and how they inform and affect daily interactions with those around us. Men are typically expected to be independent and unemotional, strong and silent, except when aggressive and competitive. Struggling with measuring up to this very narrow and unfulfilling notion of masculinity can be extremely difficult and dispiriting. Yet society often frowns upon boys who express frustration, resentment, or sadness over struggles of any kind, particularly with gender and masculinity. Everyone has feelings, but boys think they need to hide them in order to earn and prove their manhood. As a result, parents and adults don't realize when something is wrong, and boys are forced to suffer on their own. Unfortunately, boys don't realize that by trying to prove their manhood through conventional and stereotypical behaviors and attitudes, they're only making themselves unhappy.

If we learn about the wide range of male sexuality, sexual identities, and notions of masculinity, we can become happier with ourselves. We can become more comfortable with our own sense of maleness and better able to relate to other people, including other men across the entire spectrum of masculinity and sexuality. This increased sense of comfort with and acceptance for ourselves and others will makes us better men. A man who strives to be the best person he can be, accepts himself, and accepts others in all their variety and difference is indeed a "real man."

CHAPTER 1

MYTHS OF MANLINESS

All your life you've been told how to act. In fact, parents and teachers tell you what to do on a daily basis. Hard as it can be to accept this kind of intrusive attention, they're doing their best to raise you right. Obviously, they expect a certain standard of behavior. Even your friends and complete strangers expect you to behave a certain way; since you're a boy, they assume you'll act like one.

Walk Like a Man

But what does it mean to "act like a boy"? Most likely, you already have a very strong idea of what "typical" guy behavior involves. To name a few conventional things, boys—and

men—participate in sports, enjoy the outdoors, and love cars. We call these gender roles, and they encompass certain interests, attitudes, and activities that "prove" the gender appropriateness of someone's behavior. Gender roles aren't based on nature, but on culture. There's nothing biologically inherent in males that pushes them toward competitive athletics and muscle cars. Instead, it's a

Society expects boys to enjoy sports. But there's no reason why guys, even athletes, can't also be interested in other activities, like reading, art, dancing, gardening, or poetry.

culture's both subtle and overt messages about what men should be interested in that provides the push.

Still, these gender expectations are buried deep in your subconscious; all your life, you've been conditioned to obey them. They're easy to accept as natural truths, but these "notions of manliness" are not biological laws. They are social custom. Nevertheless, we tend to punish those who don't follow accepted gender roles. We judge people based on how well they fit the mold. Yet just as it's wrong to make assumptions about a person based on his or her race, ethnicity, religion, or age, it's equally wrong to make assumptions about a person based upon his or her gender. In making such prejudiced assumptions and judgments, we strip away a person's individuality and instead demand that he or she conform to a stereotype.

Stereotypes make it impossible to really know a person. In this way, they limit our view of the world and the people in it. They hurt our relationships, but stereotypes also affect our personal development. There is constant social, familial, and cultural pressure on boys to act "manly." This pressure chains us to the

Most boys believe they must be physically strong in order to be considered manly. They think the best way to prove their masculinity is by constantly asserting their strength and challenging others in physical contests.

behavior that's deemed "appropriate" for boys, or else we risk exclusion. Every man and boy alive has experienced this burden. By examining some common stereotypes of masculinity, we can better understand how they restrict our individuality and how we can break free of them.

Masculine or Feminine?

In past centuries, young males showed characteristics such as responsibility to prove they were no longer children and had earned the right to be viewed and treated as men. They might take on a larger share of chores around the farm or find work to help supplement the family income. In other words, manhood was considered the opposite of childhood. Young men feared being perceived as too childlike or babyish.

Today, young men feel they must prove their masculinity by exhibiting traditionally masculine traits, such as strength, competitiveness, and machismo (being "macho"). While young males of ages passed feared being viewed as childish, today's young males are more likely to fear being viewed as "effeminate" or "girly." They are less concerned with developing into good men than in proving beyond a shadow of a doubt their conventional masculinity. But adopting the attitudes and behaviors of a stereotyped masculinity is not at all the same thing as being or becoming a man.

In our society, every personality trait is stereotypically labeled as masculine or feminine. Boys are supposed to be independent, unemotional, brave, competitive, and aggressive. In a word: strong. We're conditioned to believe that girls, on the other hand, are dependent, emotional, sensitive, nurturing, and passive. Girls are expected to be "soft," even "weak." The stereotypes don't end there. Activities, hobbies, interests, careers, favorite TV shows, movies, clothing, and even colors: almost everything in life is categorized as masculine or feminine. For example, ballet is widely considered a feminine activity. Any boy that enjoys watching or dancing ballet is not following accepted gender roles and might be labeled as "girly."

No doubt, you know someone, probably many people, who don't fit these gender stereotypes. Maybe you don't fit them either. In reality, no one does. There is some part of everyone's personality, behavior, attitudes, or interests that does not conform to traditional gender expectations. But most of us fear the humiliation that comes with being different, of not fitting in, of not measuring up. Girls with masculine interests, like auto mechanics or certain sports like football and ice hockey, may be ridiculed. But in this regard, boys have it worse. A girl would not be embarrassed to wear a pair of pants or a flannel shirt for example, but what about a boy in a skirt or a pink sweater?

In your daily life, as silly as it is, everything you do is judged as strong or weak, masculine or feminine. If you don't fall on the "right" side of that line, you risk being laughed at or worse. However, by being dishonest with yourself and others and repressing your individuality, you risk even more. You risk losing your very self.

When you avoid those interests of yours that are allegedly feminine in order to appear more stereotypically masculine, you limit the options available to you. According to the U.S. Department of Education, more than three times as many boys are involved in team sports than there are participating in any other type of after-school activity. However, girls are one and a half times more likely than boys to participate in nonathletic activities, such as student government. This study shows how the pressure to conform can force young men to pursue certain activities, like sports, even if they don't want to or have no real interest in them.

If you play sports, perhaps you've noticed boys on your team who aren't very good. Maybe they don't seem to be having fun, as if someone is forcing them to play. This is extremely common. Clearly, those boys would be much happier doing something they enjoy. They might prefer participating in the drama club, chorus, the school newspaper, or an after-school arts or foreign language club—even though others might consider them "feminine" activities. It's impossible to be happy without first being comfortable with yourself and true to your interests, passions, and talents.

Gender roles don't just dictate behavior. They dictate everything, even the way a boy looks. From a very early age, we're assaulted with unrealistic expectations for our appearance. But how do these expectations affect us? Where do they come from? And why do they exist?

The Appearance of Masculinity

We've talked about popular misconceptions of how boys are "supposed" to act, but there are also stereotypes of

At one time, long hair was considered extremely feminine. However, today it is an acceptable, and even fashionable, style for men such as Super Bowl champion quarterback Tom Brady.

how boys should look. Obviously, this pertains to clothing; it's very clear what boys can and can't wear. If someone breaks these "rules," they're looked down upon. Even though it wouldn't hurt anybody, you'd be teased if you went to school in high heels, a dress, or makeup. Yet you wouldn't even have to dress in such an obviously feminine manner to attract potentially negative attention. What if you wore a pink sweater, a bracelet or necklace, or cologne?

Many people assume that only girls worry about their bodily appearance. That's not true. Just like girls, boys believe that they must be attractive to others to be happy. Both boys and girls are given examples of attractiveness by the mass media and do their best to follow these examples. However, the men whom boys see in movies, music videos, videogames, advertisements, and TV shows are actually highly manufactured and "airbrushed" images. They are impossible to duplicate in the real world. The imperfections of actors and models are often "fixed" with makeup, costumes, and special effects. Videogame and comic book characters are entirely fantastical, the product of an artist's imagination. They have little or nothing to do with real men, real behaviors, and real bodies.

All the same, many boys have a negative body image. In other words, they aren't happy with their body because they don't measure up to these fantastical media images. Young men often have a distorted opinion of themselves; even traditionally good-looking,

It's important to remember that different cultures define masculinity in different ways. In Scotland, the kilt, a type of skirt once worn by fierce warriors, is still considered rugged and manly.

athletic boys can have a negative body image. Since they compare themselves to unrealistic-looking men in the media, they may think they aren't muscular enough, that they're too fat, or that they have too much body hair. As a result, they're unhappy. We all want to be "perfect," but we have an inaccurate idea of what that means. A Harvard University study found that college-aged men guessed that women preferred men with 20–30 pounds (9–14 kilograms) more muscle than is considered average. Ironically, in the same study, women actually preferred men closer to average.

Nevertheless, young men may take risks to obtain the "perfect" body. They might exercise obsessively, diet, fast, or use steroids. In certain cases, boys even develop eating disorders. There is no such thing as perfection. To be happy, you must be happy with yourself, as you are. We all know that's not easy. Few people are really secure with themselves.

It's important to remember, though, that masculinity is defined differently from place to place, and notions of masculinity within a culture are always shifting and changing. In Scotland, the kilt, a type of skirt, is considered a highly masculine article of clothing. It's actually manly and rugged to wear a kilt. Also, even though it's considered attractive today, muscular bodies were once considered ugly because they were associated with poor, working-class laborers (the only men likely to be muscular due to their physically demanding jobs). If you study advertising in North American magazines from the 1950s

STEROIDS AND OBSESSIVE EXERCISE

Any man, no matter how fit, can have a negative body image. Many professional baseball players have given in to pressure by using steroids and other performance-enhancing drugs. They've ruined any chance at a legacy by cheating, but they've also put their bodies at risk. Steroids can cause depression and psychosis, a severe mental condition that includes delusions and hallucinations. The user may experience extreme mood swings that can lead to violence. Users may also become infertile and experience impotence (erectile dysfunction). Their testicles may shrink, their breasts may grow, and they may go bald. Furthermore, the bulk that users gain is actually mostly due to water retention and bloating, not muscle growth at all. Clearly, steroid use is not worth it.

It's important to stay healthy, but how far is too far? The Centers for Disease Control and Prevention recommends one hour of physical activity each day, mostly aerobic, such as walking or jogging. You only need to include muscle-strengthening activities in your workout three days a week. Anything more can be dangerous, unnecessary, and extremely unhealthy.

to the present, you will see just how dramatically the "masculine ideal" has shifted over time. Every decade, a new ideal look for men is popular, leaving the majority of real men out in the cold.

Just as gender roles have changed, they will change again. And so will the body types that are considered attractive, desirable, and classically masculine or feminine. If we can remember that, we can take another step toward self-acceptance and self-confidence.

Free to Be You and Me

Our society seems to value men who are independent, stoic, unemotional, aggressive, brave, ambitious, and above all else, strong. If a young male doesn't possess these qualities, or if he possesses the supposedly "feminine" opposite qualities, other males look down on him, as if he's less of a man. But is there anything braver than being yourself, even if others make fun of you? Openly gay teenagers are bullied, and even physically attacked, by people who feel threatened by their refusal to conform to the norms of masculinity. Every day, gay teenagers show tremendous courage, far more than the cowardly but "macho" bullies who harass them.

All our lives, we worry that we'll be treated as outcasts if we don't live up to others' expectations, but if we all stopped making assumptions about each other and supported each other's individuality and difference, we'd be free to act however we wish. Keep in mind: we're all different, and the things that make us different make us important and unique. Think of all of the people you look up to. Whether it's a family member, a friend, an athlete, a teacher, an artist, or a movie star, you respect them because they're different. They're unique. They stand out. No one else is like them. They're special. Their individuality is an asset.

You don't need to borrow your manhood from someone else or from a phony, manufactured image. And you don't need to prove your manhood by picking on the supposedly "unmanly." In fact, through their cowardly and panicked actions, bullies prove only their own unmanliness. When you grow up, you will be a man, no matter how stereotypically masculine you are or are not. That is a given. The question is not whether or not you're a man, but rather what type of man you are. You must create your own ideal to live up to. You must try to be good, and goodness has no gender.

MASCULINITY IN THE MASS MEDIA

The "mass media" refers to any means of communication that reaches a large number of people. This includes television, movies, commercials, magazines, the Internet, newspapers, radio, billboards, music, comic books, and video games. Obviously, the mass media affects the way we see the world. However, we may not realize the enormous part it plays in forming our conception of gender roles.

A Manufactured Masculinity

The mass media often presents us with unrealistic and unhealthy examples of masculinity. These examples— swaggering and ultra-violent action-adventure heroes in movies and on television, misbehaving musicians, egomaniacal athletes, and others—reinforce stereotypes of what it means to "be a man." It's nearly impossible to avoid the mass media in daily life. Its constant presence affects us subconsciously. In other words, we're not even aware of the powerful effect it is having on us.

The mass media always has a bias. When we experience the mass media, we see life through the eyes of the people who created it and the motivations that drove them. For example, radio DJs feature songs that they are directed to play by management. Station managers are intent on reaching the largest possible audience by providing music that is not too original, idiosyncratic, challenging, or controversial. They don't want to risk alienating listeners, but instead draw them in with music that is fresh and popular and "safe." Magazine editors choose subjects that they think reinforce the self-image of their readers and mesh with the audience that the magazine's advertisers are trying to reach. Through advertising, corporations craft images based upon what they think appeals to consumers and sells product. Television shows and movies are made to appeal to what is thought to be a broad general audience of conservative, conventional tastes.

All of these mass media products—advertising images, music, text, and film and television—are based upon an appeal to a large audience that is believed to desire new versions of old, safe, comfortable things. The mass audience is thought to want something new but not different. It is thought that consumers of mass media don't want their basic conceptions to be challenged, but rather reinforced. This is why so much of the mass media seems so uniform. It is also why it often traffics in blatant, unquestioned, easily recognizable gender stereotypes. If we're not aware that the mass media is always biased to a certain degree, particularly toward conventional gender stereotypes, we may think that its version of reality is true to life. When that happens, we accept media bias as fact, and its point of view becomes our own.

However, the mass media can only control us if we're unaware of how it operates. By learning how it affects us, we can safely enjoy the mass media without absorbing its stereotypes about "normal" and "acceptable" gender behavior.

Advertising, a type of mass media, uses alluring, unrealistic images of men and women to sell products. These unrealistic images also undermine ordinary people's self-image.

Profanity, Sex, and Violence

Most forms of mass media have ratings boards that judge content for objectionable material, such as sex or profanity, and classify it based on the age group that can appropriately enjoy it. That way, parents can decide whether or not a film, TV show, video game, or album will be suitable just by looking at the ratings.

In the mass media, violence is generally considered more acceptable than sex or profanity. A film, for example, can receive an R rating simply for bad language, while a PG-13 movie gets away with murder, literally. Violent films may receive an R rating in certain cases, but only if the violence is sexual and/or very extreme. However, a single instance of the use of certain obscenities or nonsexual nudity can earn a film an R rating.

It's unclear if ratings boards reflect the general attitudes of society or help form them. But whichever the case, both ratings boards and the general public now find violence, even extreme and meaningless screen violence, to be less objectionable than sex. This is true even if the sex is between a lawfully married man and woman. As a society, we're more comfortable with violence—something that is horrible and criminal in real life—than we are with sexuality.

Yet sex is a normal, healthy, and vital aspect of human life, whereas violence is aberrant and toxic to society. Sex can have negative consequences, but countless responsible adults enjoy healthy and enriching sex lives. Sex has the power to both create life and express, sustain, and expand feelings of love for one's partner. What's objectionable about any of this? Are nudity and profanity really more dangerous to people's minds and destructive to the social fabric than a relentless parade of violent onscreen

Violent imagery and themes in mass media are far more tolerated by society than are sexual themes and images. Even the most gruesome and depraved violent movies will usually receive a less restrictive rating than films that contain a single sex scene.

images and actions? Violence is dangerous. It always results in physical harm, and it's illegal. Why do we think that violence is less obscene than sex or bad words and

They may entertain us, but action heroes aren't always the best role models. The heroism of "real men" lies in the fulfilment of their daily family responsibilities: making bag lunches for the kids, washing the dinner dishes, and reading bedtime stories.

less deserving of restrictions? It's the very definition of "objectionable."

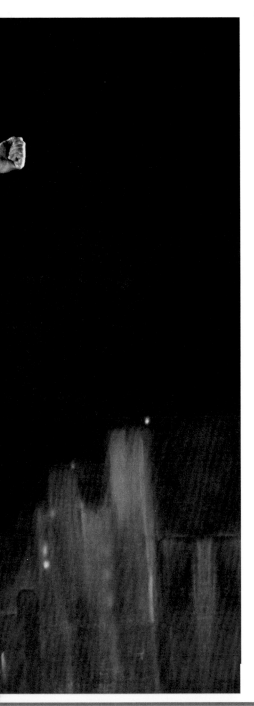

Action Heroes

To understand how implicit messages are delivered in the mass media, we should examine one of the most beloved character types among male viewers: the action hero. Action-adventure (including war, Western, and superhero) is one of the most popular entertainment genres, or categories, among men.

It's no surprise then that the main character in an action-adventure movie, TV show, or video game is nearly always male and always strong. He's also independent; he may have a partner, but most likely he works alone and sometimes outside the law. He doesn't take advice from others, and he never compromises his beliefs. He's handsome. He uses violence to resolve conflict. Sometimes the main character is smart and witty, but he is always brave and strong first and foremost. Action heroes embody almost every masculine stereotype. We may look up to these characters, and may even try to be like them. After all, what's wrong with being brave and strong?

Absolutely nothing. Bravery, integrity, independence, and strength are all very valuable qualities. But there are also many important qualities that an action hero doesn't typically exhibit. These include patience, kindness, compassion, empathy, consideration, gentleness, and intelligence. Action heroes also have many negative characteristics, such as stubbornness, recklessness, and an itchy trigger finger. We may wish that action heroes were real, but they're not; they're two-dimensional. An action hero may be the perfect man to stop terrorists from blowing up the Statue of Liberty, but he would never make a good husband or father in the real world. Being a good and decent family man is a far harder, nobler, and more heroic task than any encountered by a macho—and entirely fictional—action hero.

In the mass media we see only a fraction of the real lives and actual life experiences occurring in the world beyond the movie, television, and computer screen. We don't often see real-life examples of heroism, so we equate heroism with the cartoonlike Hollywood version. In the real world, heroism is measured differently. Doctors and nurses save real lives every day with their intelligence, education, skill, and competence, not their

UNCOOL BOYS, FAMOUS MEN

Straight As will make your parents happy, but they might not gain you popularity in school. However, teenage popularity has little to do with your accomplishments as an adult. In fact, many famous men and women were unpopular teenagers.

It may not surprise you that Bill Gates, cofounder of Microsoft, was a nerd in high school. Though his intelligence and ingenuity didn't earn him social status then, now he is one of the most influential men of our time. Actor Samuel L. Jackson, a stereotypically masculine pop-culture icon and action film star, has loved comic books since he was a little boy. This is a passion that is usually associated with geeks who have no physical aptitude. Seven-time Tour de France winner Lance Armstrong didn't fit in at high school because he was more interested in cycling than football. Back then, cycling wasn't nearly as well-regarded in the United States as it is now, and it wasn't considered a very masculine sport.

We can get so caught up in the tangled web of high school power dynamics and social status-seeking that we may think nothing will ever change. Of course, that's not true. Moreover, as is the case with these now-famous and successful men, the qualities that set you apart from others will soon become your chief assets. After all, it's impossible to be great if you are just the same as everyone else.

physical strength. You don't have to be muscle-bound to be a hero. In fact, to be a real hero, you don't even have to be manly or a man at all.

Objectifying Women

It might seem odd, but much can be learned about society's notions of masculinity by studying the mass media's portrayal of women. Young men and women are assumed to like different types of music, movies, TV shows, and magazines. When it wishes to attract a male audience, the mass media tends to appeal to what is assumed to be typical male interests—big guns, fast cars, extreme violence, and beautiful women. The women in male-oriented mass media tend to conform to cultural stereotypes of femininity and/or conventional male fantasies. So the female characters tend to be beautiful, passive, submissive, unintelligent sexual play-things. Sometimes they conform to men's most dark fears and are evil temptresses bent on attacking the charac-ter's manhood and undermining his authority and masculinity.

Heterosexual men, the only kind of men the mass media really concerns itself with, find women attractive. Men's media responds to that attraction by objectifying women. In other words, women are presented as mere objects without intelligence, selfhood, substance, or free will. Think of the damsel in distress, the disposable love interest in an action movie, or the faceless gyrating bodies of female dancers in a male musician's music video. These actresses or models, real people in the real world, have been reduced to attractive bodies. The characters they play are used, stared at, or put in danger, and they always need men to make them whole.

Just as the mass media influences our concept of masculinity, it also affects our concept of femininity. Perhaps if men are supposed to be like action heroes, women should be like the silent, subordinate, scantily clad actress the action hero rescues and seduces. We may begin to believe this extremely limited view of what women are as reality and forget the fact that girls and women are actual people. They are fully rounded, complex, thinking and feeling human beings. As such, they deserve to be treated with respect. Boys and men don't need to follow the examples set out for them in the mass media, and neither do girls and women.

Famous Men

We've talked a lot about the mass media's examples of the masculine ideal. However, there are popular and successful celebrities who don't fit typical gender roles at all. Though not fulfilling the masculine ideal, these men still enjoy success and fame.

Leading men aren't always buff and handsome. In comedies, the most important quality is funniness; looks don't matter nearly as much. Dave Chappelle, Will Ferrell, Michael Cera, Jack Black, and Zach Galifianakis are more average looking than Brad Pitt, Bradley Cooper, or Denzel

Will Ferrell isn't a masculine stereotype. He is neither movie star handsome nor muscle-bound. But he is funny, talented, successful, and beloved, and he seems to be a great dad.

Washington, but their characters are just as likeable, if not more so. If these comedic actors had tried to conform to gender norms and play sports instead of pursuing their interests in comedy, writing, and performing, our culture would be far less rich—and much less entertaining. It doesn't matter that these men aren't muscle-bound gods and don't have classic matinee idol good looks. That makes them easier to relate to. They show us that we can be successful by being ourselves, even if we aren't action heroes or gym rats.

Of course, you don't need money and fame to be a good person. Every day, good men live their lives without receiving any fanfare from others. We can learn just as much, if not more, about being good men from firefighters, policemen, doctors, nurses, judges, teachers, parents, and so on.

CHAPTER 3

BOYS AND GIRLS: A DOUBLE STANDARD

W hen you see a parent pushing a baby in a stroller, how do you know if the baby is a boy or a girl? Many parents dress their babies in different colors depending on sex: blue for boys or pink for girls. Passersby might say, "He's going to be so big," about a son, or "He'll be a heartbreaker." For daughters, they'd say, "She's so petite," and "She's so pretty." The boys play with cars and trains, while the girls get dolls and tea sets. It's easy to see that from a very early age, boys and girls are treated completely differently based on their sex.

Nature Vs. Nurture

Boys and girls are different. Boys are generally expected to be masculine, strong, active, and unemotional, and girls the opposite. But are boys and girls born that way, or are they taught? This is a very common question, and an important one. Nature vs. nurture is the debate over the

DOUBLE STANDARDS AND SPLIT SELVES

When it comes to boys and girls, society has a double standard, or a different set of rules for one group than for the other. For example, parents typically give their sons more freedom than their daughters, but trust them less. This paradox exists because many parents think boys need to "sow wild oats" before settling down into responsible adulthood. Not only is this unfair, it's also harmful. When we define people based on their gender, we affect the way they define themselves.

In their book *The Courage to Raise Good Men*, authors Olga Silverstein and Beth Rashbaum note that our culture forces boys and girls to "halve" themselves. In other words, they are forced to ignore the half of their personality that doesn't fit gender stereotypes. As a result, they can only hope to become half of a well-rounded human being. Clearly, by upholding this double standard, we ignore our true selves and limit our potential for happiness.

This double standard affects us all. Girls experience discrimination throughout their entire lives, but boys' problems are often ignored. There's no point in discussing who has it "worse" because uneven treatment hurts us all. Until we're equal, we will never be whole human beings.

importance of a person's inherited qualities (the qualities he or she is born with, or "nature") versus the person's experiences and environment ("nurture," as in upbringing) in determining personality and behavior. Nature vs. nurture is discussed in regards to many different subjects, including gender roles. In this case, is it a person's biological sex (nature) that determines behavior, or is it the gender roles he or she learns from culture, society, and other people (nurture)?

Many people believe that boys are born with traditionally masculine interests and traits, but that isn't the case. Some boys are genuinely drawn to cars, trucks, and trains, but others are taught to be interested in them by society.

Most people think that men and women are different because their brains are "wired" differently. Maybe you've heard that girls are quicker to learn than boys, or that boys are better at playing sports because they're naturally good at tracking movement. However, scientific research shows that boys' and girls' brains are almost completely identical. In an article in the *Observer*, Lise Elliot, an associate professor at Chicago Medical School, said, "All the mounting evidence indicates these ideas about hard-wired differences between male and female brains are wrong."

Our sex is determined by our physical traits, specifically reproductive organs. That makes us either male or female. We're born with a sex, but according to scientific research, we're not born with any knowledge that boys and girls should act differently. What determines our gender—the behaviors and attitudes that are considered masculine or feminine and appropriate to males or females—is our environment. Our families, our friends, our culture, our society assign us a gender. This then determines how we're defined, treated, and taught. Therefore, the common emotional and behavioral differences between boys and girls are not caused by their birth or sex (nature), but by the way they're taught and the gender expectations placed upon them (nurture). Gendered behavior is learned; it is not automatically determined by biology or one's sex.

We also know that gender roles are not "hard-wired" in our brains because they differ from culture to culture. In modern Western culture, we recognize two genders, masculine and feminine, but some cultures recognize more than two. Oman, a country on the Arabian Peninsula,

Gender is fluid and difficult to strictly categorize. Many men who identify as heterosexual ("straight") also enjoy makeup and cross-dressing. Many gay men are extremely macho. There are no absolutes when it comes to gender identity.

acknowledges a third gender, *xaniths*—biological males who live, dress, and are treated as women. Other societies even legally recognize four genders.

How can we account for these "extra" genders if we're all born either masculine or feminine? At birth, boys and girls are the same. They have a sex (male or female), but they are not yet gendered. They have the potential to develop a mix of "masculine" and "feminine" traits according to their personality and their environmental influences.

Gender roles are not biological but based on a complex set of influences that differ from culture to culture.

It is society that labels any particular trait as masculine or feminine, but there is nothing inherent in that trait that is truly gendered. Nurturing and compassion are labeled as feminine, but there's nothing inherently feminine about them, and many men have these traits. Similarly aggression and physical strength are labeled masculine, but there's nothing inherently masculine about them, and many women exhibit these traits as well. It is just that from a very young age, male and female children are taught by society—explicitly and

Nowadays, women are just as likely as men to work outside the home and earn income for the family. Yet many women still earn less pay than men for the exact same work.

implicitly—what is appropriate to their sex. And not conforming oneself to these traits exposes one to ridicule, ostracism (being separated and cast off from the group), and disapproval.

When they're born, boys and girls are the same. As they grow up, our society teaches them to be different. Those differences make it more difficult for men and women to relate to each other. Instead of searching for

differences, we should look for similarities, so that we can bring boys and girls together instead of driving another wedge between them.

Fathers and Mothers

Parents buy into traditional gender roles. It's common for them to give their sons plenty of space so that they'll eventually be strong and independent enough to support themselves, and later a wife and family. Daughters, however, are often kept close, overprotected, and sheltered. It doesn't matter if girls are independent, since they're expected to have a husband one day who'll protect and take care of them just as their father did.

Obviously, this outlook is extremely old-fashioned. In this day and age, if you get married, your spouse will likely have a job. She may even make more money than you. You and your partner may never have children, or else you might never be married at all. Marriage can be a wonderful thing, but it's also possible to be single and very happy and fulfilled. At any rate, it's wrong to expect that all boys will get married one day and have to work to support their family, just as it is wrong to assume a girl doesn't need to learn the life skills necessary for adult independence and success.

Yet parents still treat their sons like future heads of household. It doesn't start that way. At some point, parents decide that they should stop "babying" their sons. They suddenly become more careful about showing affection and start to give their sons more space. It seems as if parents are bracing themselves, getting ready for when their sons will suddenly change from happy little boys into sullen and willful teenagers. Teenage boys, they think, will have to face problems on their own, so they shouldn't be pampered. Of course, girls become teenagers, too. But parents keep their daughters close in order to protect them (from, among other things, teenage boys). Some parents fear that their daughters will never be strong enough to face life's challenges on their own, without the help and guidance of a man.

It's easy for boys to pick up on the sudden changes in their parents' behavior. Boys know that they're expected to be independent, and they do their best to live up to those expectations. As you grow up, it's natural to crave more independence, since you're almost an adult and you'll live by yourself someday, whether or not you get married. But keep in mind that your relationship with your parents is changing, not ending. You don't have to choose between total parental involvement and none at all. Nor do you have to stop showing warmth and affection to each other.

There are certain things you'll want to do for yourself, and that's fine, but your family will still be there to support you and give guidance. It may not seem like it, but your family is a valuable asset whether you're a child or an adult. It's important to include your parents in your life, even if you don't sit on their lap or hold their hands anymore.

Understanding Emotions

Boys and girls experience the same emotions, but boys tend to ignore, hide, and repress theirs. Many boys think they're only "allowed" to show supposedly masculine emotions, like anger and pride. They must keep supposedly feminine emotions, like affection, love, or sadness, bottled up inside. By hiding their "softer" side, these boys think that they'll appear stronger and more typically masculine to others. However, it's difficult enough to understand emotions when one is open to them. By ignoring them altogether, boys make their problems worse. They stunt their development as men and as thinking, feeling human beings.

Everyone has feelings; just because men don't show them, doesn't mean they don't exist. Most men are afraid to be vulnerable. They're worried they'll be ridiculed for being "too soft," "too feminine." Yet it takes courage, not weakness, to acknowledge your emotions, to accept them, and to show them in public.

Emotions can be complicated. Many boys avoid talking about their feelings, even when they want to. As a result, they may not be able to identify what they, and other people, are feeling. That can make it extremely difficult for

It may not always be easy, and sometimes it may be awkward or embarrassing, but speaking to a parent or other trusted adult about your feelings and problems can go a long way to making you feel better and resolving any difficulties.

boys to connect with another person, such as a family member, friend, or significant other. Boys who can't emotionally connect with people end up feeling lonely, which can lead to depression. In addition to hurting your relationships, depression can increase the risk of substance abuse, physical illness, and even suicide.

When boys repress their emotions, keeping them bottled up, they may begin to feel frustrated. That bottled-up frustration can suddenly burst out, take control, and affect behavior. Some people may even become violent in response to their frustration. A study conducted by sociology professors Kristi Williams, Debra Umberson, and

Kristin Anderson found that domestic violence often occurs among men who repress their emotions. Of course, repressed emotion is not enough to make a person violent. But this study shows that emotions need to be understood and expressed before they fester and become unhealthy.

Adults can't always guess that their child is repressing his emotions, so they think nothing's wrong. The only way they'll ever know is if their son speaks up for himself. There are many places to turn. It may seem like adults won't understand, or that no one has gone through what you're experiencing, but that's not true. Everyone has feelings, and everyone struggles to understand them.

You can talk to your parents, an aunt or uncle, a teacher you trust, an older brother, or a guidance counselor. Friends are great, too, but maybe you don't feel comfortable talking about feelings with other guys. Girls are typically more comfortable with emotion, so a female friend might be able to help. The best solutions are always found through discussion, and talking can make you feel much better. Remember: feelings are a good thing. Given free expression, they are ultimately a source of strength.

Myths and Facts

Myth

Blue has always been the color for boys, and pink has always been the color for girls.

Fact

Actually, it used to be the opposite. Up until the 1940s, people considered pink to be masculine. Blue was seen as light and airy and not strong enough for men. There weren't distinctions between colors for men or women at all until the late 1800s.

Myth

"Feminine" behavior and activities can transform a straight man into a gay man.

Fact

No one event "makes" someone gay. Sexual orientation is extremely complex and is usually present at a very early age.

Myth

Heterosexual men have always had problems with homosexual and bisexual men.

Fact

Visible gay subcultures first emerged in urban areas in the 1850s, and at that time, there was a casual coexistence between gay and straight men.

CHAPTER 4

GLBT LIFE

The acronym GLBT refers to gay, lesbian, bisexual, and transgendered people. Gay men and lesbian women are also known as homosexuals, which means that they're attracted to people of the same sex. A transgendered person is someone who dresses or lives as a member of the opposite sex, whether through cross-dressing, hormone therapy, surgery, or other means. "GLBT" is meant to include many different cultures whose identities are based on sexuality and gender. It is sometimes used as a general term for nonheterosexual people (people who aren't "straight").

It is not known how many GLBT people there are. The 2010 census marked the first time that same-sex married couples were counted in the once-a-decade population count. At that time, the District of Columbia and five states—Connecticut, Iowa, Massachusetts, Vermont, and New Hampshire—had legalized same-sex marriage. States that recognize same-sex marriages performed in other states but do not grant same-sex marriage licenses include Rhode

The GLBT movement is gaining ground in the battle for equal treatment, but there is still a long way to go.

Island and Maryland. California, Colorado, Hawaii, Maine, Maryland, Nevada, Oregon, Rhode Island, Wisconsin, Illinois, New Jersey, and Washington have created legal unions for same-sex couples. These offer many of the rights and responsibilities of marriage under the laws of those jurisdictions. As legalization of gay marriage and civil unions spreads to more states, more accurate Census figures are likely to be collected regarding the number of gay people, gay couples, and families headed by a gay single parent or two same-sex parents. Interpretation of previous Census data suggests that same-sex couples lived in virtually every U.S. county. This means that there are same-sex couples everywhere in the United States. Many are afraid to "come out," to reveal their sexual orientation to others. They are worried that they'll be mistreated, oppressed, socially cast out, or physically hurt.

GLBT people lead lives that challenge traditional gender roles, which can make conservative heterosexuals uncomfortable. As a result, we have many inaccurate ideas about what it is to be GLBT and what GLBT people are like. Unfortunately, prejudice and homophobia, an unreasonable fear or hatred of homosexuality, can keep heterosexuals from ever meeting a GLBT person. Luckily, education can help. A secondary school in London, England, reported to the *Guardian*, a British newspaper, that it had eliminated homophobic bullying by teaching lessons about people in history who were persecuted for being gay. This example proves that as we become more familiar with GLBT culture, we realize that not only is there nothing to be afraid of, but also that the GLBT community actually provides examples of heroism, courage, decency, and strength to celebrate and emulate.

A Brief History

We learn little to nothing about the history of GLBT people in school, and there is too much to discuss in one book. Likely, many people are not even aware that there is such a thing as GLBT history. Of course, they have not always identified themselves as "GLBT," but there have always been homosexuals and transgendered people, and they have affected world history in various ways.

Homosexual relationships were extremely common in ancient Greece. In fact, ancient Greeks didn't even have words for "homosexual" or "heterosexual." There was no distinction. They defined relationships based on age and status, not sex or gender, and attraction was considered a matter of taste, not morality. Many famous ancient Greeks were homosexual or bisexual, including Alexander the Great, one of the most successful military commanders of all time.

Homosexuality has been accepted in many different times and places. But by and large, Western culture has criminalized same-sex relationships since the twelfth century CE. Most Europeans believed GLBT lifestyles were unnatural. As they explored and colonized the rest of the world, however, they were surprised to find nonheterosexuals all over. In fact, examples of homosexuality have been documented on every continent.

In America, GLBT people have often been simultaneously discriminated against and ignored. For a long time, it was extremely uncommon for any homosexual or bisexual person to be open about his or her sexual orientation for fear of being ostracized, abused, and physically attacked.

The Stonewall Rebellion

In the early morning of June 27, 1969, New York City police conducted a raid at the Stonewall Inn, a popular

bar for homosexuals. Police raided gay bars regularly, often only to harass the clientele. However, that night, for the first time, the customers fought back.

This conflict, known as the Stonewall Rebellion, was a major turning point for gay rights in America. Gay men and lesbian women had had enough. Up until then, most

The rainbow flag of the GLBT movement represents all people living together–regardless of race, religion, ethnicity, sex, gender, or orientation–celebrating their differences while living in perfect harmony.

homosexuals had kept their orientation a secret. After the Stonewall Rebellion, however, many individuals realized that there were countless others experiencing the same oppression and injustice as them. Homosexuals united, organized, and began openly protesting for equal rights. It was the birth of the gay pride movement.

HIV and AIDS

In 1981, the Centers for Disease Control and Prevention (CDC) reported roughly two hundred gay men with symptoms of various rare diseases, including Kaposi's sarcoma (KS), a type of cancer. It was not known at the time, but this was the beginning of the AIDS epidemic.

"AIDS" stands for acquired immunodeficiency syndrome, and it is caused by HIV, the human immunodeficiency virus. HIV and AIDS attack your immune system so that your body can't fight infections. Initially, there was no treatment, and hundreds of thousands of people died. HIV/AIDS is transmitted through bodily fluids. Everyone is potentially susceptible, no matter his or her race, gender, or sexual orientation, but the most widely publicized cases in the early years of the epidemic were those of gay men. The general public feared the disease and blamed gay people. Initially, the American government largely ignored the outbreak.

The GLBT community fought back. AIDS activists protested the mistreatment of gay men and AIDS patients. Knowing that the disease could be transmitted sexually, the GLBT community pioneered safe-sex practices for hetero- and homosexual people alike. Thanks to many dedicated activists, the general public became aware of the true risk factors and causes of HIV/AIDS. Since then, there have been huge advances in drug therapy and treatment, but still no cure.

GLBT Today

GLBT people have become more and more visible in popular culture. Mainstream movies and TV shows openly address topics of GLBT mistreatment and discrimination. But they also depict GLBT people living perfectly ordinary, healthy, and rewarding lives, including in their roles as parents. There are also many prominent homosexual actors and TV personalities, like comedian/talk-show host Ellen Degeneres and actor Neil Patrick Harris, who speak out for GLBT rights. Angelina Jolie and Lady Gaga are both bisexual. This relatively new level of visibility has brought greater familiarity and acceptance of GLBT people than ever before in the United States.

There have been some recent significant advances in GLBT rights. In 2009, President Barack Obama signed the Matthew Shepard and James Byrd, Jr. Hate Crime Prevention Act (HCPA) into law. A hate crime is a violent crime in which the victim is chosen because of his or her actual or perceived race, religion, nationality, gender, sexual orientation, gender identity, or disability. The law aims to prevent hate crimes by providing more funding to their investigations and to hate crime awareness. The HCPA is named after two hate crime victims. Matthew Shepard was a gay man who was tortured and murdered in Laramie, Wyoming, in 1998. James Byrd Jr., an African American man, was dragged to death behind a pickup truck in Jasper, Texas, by three white men also in 1998.

Gay rights activists and their supporters protest the kind of homophobia that led to the murder of twenty-one-year-old Matthew Shepard.

The fight for GLBT rights is far from over, though. Same-sex sexual activity is still illegal in many countries. Although now legal in the United States, it was outlawed in some states until a Supreme Court ruling in 2003, *Lawrence v.*

FITZROY GREEN

Texas. Laws are different from state to state, but in most places, same-sex marriage is illegal. Same-sex couples are also not allowed to adopt children in certain states. Furthermore, bisexual and transgendered people have not enjoyed even the limited integration into and acceptance by mainstream society that gays and lesbians have. Clearly, we have a long way to go.

Common Misconceptions

There are many stereotypes, myths, and misconceptions about GLBT people that are commonly accepted by the

The stereotype of the lonely, depressed, fearful, or promiscuous gay man does not correspond to the larger reality. There are many gay and bisexual young men living happy, fulfilling lives, full of love, friendship, family, and community.

general population, for lack of real information and first-hand experience with gay people. The general public isn't adequately exposed to GLBT culture. Unfortunately there isn't always a line of communication open for GLBT people to express themselves and reveal the realities of their daily lives.

Some heterosexuals believe that GLBT people choose

their sexual orientation. That's not true. Ritch Savin-Williams, professor of human development at Cornell University, interviewed a large group of gay and bisexual male teenagers and found that 80 percent experienced their first same-sex attractions before puberty. These boys all believed that their attractions began so early, even before they knew what it meant to be gay, that it must be natural. They felt they were born gay; they didn't "become" gay or "choose" to become gay. Furthermore, boys identified themselves as gay or bisexual even if they'd never had sex. Sexual orientation is not based on actions or choice, but on how a person feels inside.

The truth is, no one knows what determines a person's sexual orientation. Some research suggests that it could be determined before birth. Sexual orientation usually develops before puberty, but it can also change through a person's life. A person may be attracted to men at some point in life and women at another. We do know that sexual orientation isn't chosen and that no one event makes a person gay. Still, some heterosexuals are afraid that homosexuals will try to "turn them gay." They shouldn't be afraid. Not only is there nothing wrong with being homosexual, it's impossible to change a person's orientation by force or persuasion.

It's also impossible to know a person's sexual orientation just by looking at him or her. We may think that gay men are effeminate and that lesbians are always masculine, but those are just simplistic stereotypes. As we've said, most individuals have a combination of masculine and feminine traits whether they're straight, gay, or bisexual. In fact, Savin-Williams found that one in ten gay or bisexual teenagers were completely "masculine." You'd never tell their orientation just by studying their appearance, speech, mannerisms, bearing, or behavior. We can only know if they tell us.

These common misconceptions about GLBT people seem harmless, but they do great damage by pushing uninformed people farther from the truth. This kind of ignorance is a gateway to bigotry, fear, hatred, and violence.

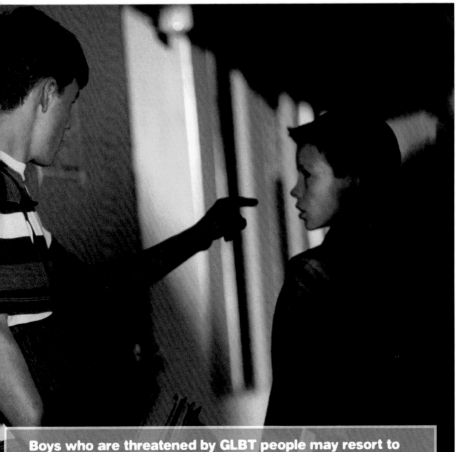

Boys who are threatened by GLBT people may resort to bullying and sexual harassment. They react with fear and confusion to anything that is different from them, and this fear makes them lash out.

Sexual Harassment

Some boys feel uncomfortable interacting with GLBT people. As we've said, GLBT culture is hardly discussed in schools, so heterosexual boys may not have any real-life experiences with someone who is gay. In this absence of information and experience, they may begin to believe stereotypes. Since GLBT people don't always follow

 DEPRESSION AND COPING

Many gay or bisexual boys may be forced to discover their sexuality alone in an unfriendly environment. As a result, they could feel alienated and become depressed. Depression is an illness characterized by unshakeable sadness, discouragement, loss of self-worth, and loss of interest in preferred activities. It can be a temporary reaction to typical adolescent stress, or it can be caused by an upsetting event, like a breakup with a girlfriend or boyfriend or the death of a relative. A family history of depression can also put teens at risk.

Of course, anyone can become depressed, no matter his or her sexual orientation. According to the U.S. Department of Health and Human Services, about one in five young people will experience depression before they become adults. It can be very dangerous and, in extreme cases, even lead to suicide.

There is treatment, though. Medication and therapy are both effective. If you think you or someone you know might be depressed, tell someone. Parents, teachers, or guidance counselors can help find professional care. If you have no one else, the Boys Town National Hotline is open 24/7 to talk: 1-800-448-3000. Remember that you're not alone, and above all else don't lose hope.

traditional gender roles, straight boys may feel like their values are being threatened. This may make them confused or angry. They could resort to bullying in order to reassert themselves and the supposed superiority or rightness of heterosexuality and traditional notions of masculinity.

Many boys bully others who don't follow masculine gender roles. Sexual harassment is bullying or intimidation of a sexual nature. Insulting or threatening a person because of his or her sexual orientation is considered sexual harassment. Bullies should think twice before victimizing someone because sexual harassment is illegal and subject to criminal punishment.

"Gay"

The word "gay" has come to mean something more than "homosexual." Boys and girls use "gay" to describe things as stupid, lame, or uncool. According to a study by the American Association of University Women, boys consider being called "gay" the worst possible insult.

Most likely, people who use "gay" in this context are unaware that they're disrespecting gay people. It's easy to see how redefining "gay" as "stupid" can upset somebody, though. Anyone would be bothered if a word they used to identify themselves—like their name, race, ethnicity, religion, or orientation—was used as an insult, especially an insult that implies something is weak, inadequate, contemptible, pathetic, or weird. It would make them feel as if their very being and essence were being insulted. We all like to joke around with our friends, but we should be

Being part of a warm and supportive group of friends can help prevent any feelings of isolation, sadness or depression. Friends will help you realize you are not alone, an outcast, or unloved.

careful about the words we use and make sure they do not hurt anyone intentionally or unintentionally.

For Gay or Bisexual Young Men

It's common for gay males to experience their first same-sex attractions at an early age, but it may take time before they acknowledge those attractions and consider themselves gay. These boys might think they're going through a phase. They might fear being gay, assuming their life will become more difficult and they'll be rejected and shunned by friends and family. They may not be able to identify with other homosexuals, especially if they've been taught that homosexuality is immoral or aberrant. It can be even more difficult and confusing for bisexual boys to identify their feelings and make sense of why they feel attracted to both girls and guys and whether that is normal or abnormal.

Stereotypical examples of both gay and bisexual boys can sometimes paint a bleak picture. If they're not shown as flamboyant and effeminate, they're depicted as moody, depressed, and suicidal. We may start to believe that neither homosexual nor bisexual teens can live normal lives. They

can, and they do every day. Even if they're bullied, both gay and bisexual boys can be happy. In fact, they tend to be more resilient and considerate than those who aren't bullied.

Gay teenagers can have as many friends, or more, as straight teenagers. Young gay males tend to have a more

If the time feels right, coming out to your parents can be an intensely liberating and moving experience. Some teens are surprised by how supportive and loving their parents are during the coming-out process.

diverse group of friends, people of different races and backgrounds who don't fit mainstream stereotypes. If you're having trouble fitting in, try a different social group. There are people out there who will like you for who you are. Not everyone is a bully. You don't have to be alone.

Coming Out

It can be extremely difficult for a gay or bisexual teenager to come out. It all depends on the individual; there's no single right time that works for everybody. Although it's hard to keep your identity a secret, there's a lot to consider before deciding whether or not to come out. It can be risky. If you're unsure, think about the pros and cons. If you decide to come out, it's important to choose the right person to confide in. If you're afraid, but need to get it off of your chest, you can always first come out anonymously to a stranger. You can call the GLBT National Youth Talkline at 1-800-246-7743, or e-mail at youth@ GLBTNationalHelpCenter.org.

There's also nothing wrong with keeping your orientation secret for a while if you're not sure how people will react. Always remember: keeping your orientation secret is not the same as being ashamed. It's most important that you protect yourself and come out only when you feel ready, when you feel safe and secure.

Role Models

Provided with real examples of GLBT people, teens may realize that they're part of a large group of people and may begin to feel more at ease with themselves. If you're ever curious, do some research. You'll discover a whole world full of interesting and important GLBT people waiting to be discovered.

Your role model doesn't even need to share the same sexual orientation, gender, or race as you. We don't always choose the people we look up to, and we aren't always sure why we look up to them in the first place. Our role models might not be perfect, and that's fine, too. There's no such thing as perfection, anyway. The important thing is that we're able to recognize our own humanity in someone great, and their greatness in ourselves.

CHAPTER 5

MASCULINITY IN DAILY INTERACTIONS

Every day, masculine gender roles influence our interactions with others. We're given certain rules of how to act appropriately for our gender, and then we are judged on whether or not we follow them "correctly." At the same time, we may judge others on whether or not they embody gender stereotypes "properly."

We've discussed why traditional gender roles are unrealistic and unhealthy. There's no good reason to adhere to them so strictly or to criticize those who don't. Traditional gender roles are only stereotypes. They disregard the nuances of personality that make an individual special. If we followed them to the letter, we'd all be the same and we'd all be very unhappy and unfulfilled, not to mention bored. We wouldn't be fully ourselves.

It's not enough to talk about it—we have to put our new knowledge into practice. That can be difficult, though. Classmates can be especially harsh when confronted with difference, and school is often a cruel place. We crave the approval of our peers, but that's not what really matters in life. Happiness doesn't come from fitting in or being superficially appreciated. It comes from loving ourselves for who we are. When we have self-respect, it's easier for us to respect others, and we'll then make valuable, genuine, and lasting friendships.

Peer Pressure

Everyone has experienced peer pressure: when friends, teammates, girlfriends, boyfriends, and/or classmates

When some teens sense that someone in their midst is different, they often gang up on him, through either verbal, emotional, or physical violence. Always strive to maintain your dignity when harassed for being different, and never stop being exactly who you are.

pressure you into doing something you don't really want to do. We want people to like us, so it's difficult to stand up to them when we feel threatened or pressured, especially if the implied punishment for not going along is social ostracism (separation and shunning). As hard as it is to say no, sometimes you have to, or else you'll end up in serious trouble and violate your principles and sense of self.

Bullies are full of fear and insecurity, which they take out on innocent victims whom they view as even weaker or more socially marginal than themselves.

It helps to think about why these other people are pressuring you. They may be trying to take a place above you on the social ladder by making you feel small. They might be afraid to do something alone, especially if they know it's wrong. They could even be worried about what you think of them. The more you give in to what someone wants from you, the more he or she will demand. Remember that good friends will always like you for exactly who you are, not for whom they want you to be.

Bullying and the Social Ladder

Boys and girls subconsciously use gender stereotypes to rank their peers. This ranking, known as the social ladder, indicates a person's status. Those on the top rung of the social ladder are privileged. Things seem to come easier for them, and they have an unexplainable power over others.

People with status, like football players and cheerleaders, are not necessarily popular, but the two words are often used interchangeably. "Status" refers to a person's social position in relation to others, while "popular" means most people regard that person favorably. A person with status is not necessarily likeable. Nevertheless, we all want status. In our desire to go up a rank, we may resort to cruelty. Many boys and girls bully in order to assert their status over someone below them on the ladder.

There are many types of bullying, such as verbal insults, pranks, public humiliation, threats, and physical violence. Boys and girls can bully by any means, including text messages or the Internet. Teens bully people to show that they're more powerful and, therefore, higher on the social ladder. Anyone can be a target, but those who don't conform to gender stereotypes are especially at risk. Even friends can be bullies. It may be hard to distinguish between bullying and joking around, but if you feel uncomfortable by something said to you, your friends have most likely crossed the line.

Ironically, bullies purposefully pick on people that they think are vulnerable. What's strong about that? Many bullies have been victims themselves. Of course, teenagers may have difficulty expressing their emotions. It's possible that when they can't express it properly, they take their frustration out on someone else. But that's no excuse. Bullying should never be allowed or tolerated. Achieving social status is completely meaningless if you have no friends (and if you've achieved your status at someone else's expense). And bullying is not a good way to make friends. Meaningful relationships are much more important than climbing the social ladder.

If you're being bullied, don't fight back. Violence is never appropriate, unless you're in a life-threatening situation. However, you should stand up for yourself. Tell the bully or bullies to leave you alone. Be assertive. Don't

CYBERBULLYING

Cyberbullying is the use of any digital or communication technology, like a cell phone or the Internet, to bully or harm another person. About 32 percent of all teenagers who use the Internet say they've been targets of cyberbullies, according to the Pew Research Center.

There are many forms of cyberbullying, including making someone's private information public, spreading rumors, posting embarrassing or doctored pictures without a person's permission, and sending threatening or aggressive e-mails, instant messages, Tweets, or text messages. Bullying is serious, whether at school or on the Internet. If you're being bullied, tell a parent, teacher, or guidance counselor.

provoke, but show that you're not willing to take their treatment. Bullies are often surprised when people stand up to them, especially in public, and you might scare them off. Also, bullies target people who are alone, so try to travel with friends.

Most of all, if you're being bullied or see someone who is being bullied, speak up. Tell an adult. It's extremely important to ask for assistance. Not only will it make your life easier, but it can also prevent the bully from targeting and hurting more people. Sometimes, admitting that you need help is the bravest thing you can do.

Social Networks

Not every interaction is face-to-face. Social network Web sites like Facebook, Myspace, and Twitter attempt to build relationships online based on shared interests. They've

Never post identifying or overly personal information, including photos, on the Internet. And if you are being cyberbullied, tell an adult immediately.

become massively popular places to socialize. They can be useful and fun, but if you aren't careful, social networking can also be hazardous.

Social network sites make private things public. Most sites have privacy controls so that you can block your personal information, but it's still possible to unknowingly put yourself at risk. When typing in a profile page, message, or status update, never write anything that could expose you to ill-intentioned strangers, such as an address, phone number, birth date, e-mail address, or your daily schedule. Criminals could use this information against you. For example, if you write a status update or Tweet that says you're going out to do something, burglars will know that your house is unguarded. A social network post that mentions your home address and the fact that you're home alone can invite predators. Giving out an e-mail address or phone number can lead to harassment.

It's even possible for an online reference to your birth date or Social Security number to lead to identity theft. Identity theft is a crime in which someone pretends to be someone else in order to steal, blackmail, or commit additional crimes. Anyone can use the information that we post to a social networking site to steal our identity. E-mail providers and online accounts use harmless tidbits, such as our favorite food or our pet's name, as identity challenges to confirm that we are whom we say we are. An identity thief can go to your e-mail provider's Web site, click the "forgot password" button, answer the security question with the information on your profile, and change your password. With your e-mail address, this person can then access your social network profiles, credit cards, bank account, and so on, not to mention read your e-mails. He or she can cause all sorts of damage.

On social networking Web sites, anyone can see photos of private moments in your life, no matter how personal or embarrassing. Even if they're locked, your friends can copy and share your photos with other people. In certain circumstances, pictures can get us into trouble. It's become common for businesses to check a job applicant's social networking profile and photos before deciding whether or not they should hire him or her. An unprofessional picture can cost you a job.

You can also be punished for what you do online. Many bosses use social networking sites to keep tabs on their employees. If they see a status update or tweet that casts their business in a bad light, they can fire you. Your parents could also check your profile to find out about your social habits and friends. It may seem like snooping, but any information you post online is fair game.

Above all else, always be skeptical of the people you meet online. Photos and a profile are not proof of people's identities, nor are they a window into their souls. They could be lying. They could look kind and harmless but actually be planning to take advantage of you. No matter how nice he or she seems, don't ever agree to meet a stranger in person.

Social networking is here to stay. So, too, are your posts. Keep in mind, when you post something online, you're creating a record that can last forever. So whenever blogging, posting, texting, or e-mailing, keep in mind that what you say in the moment can continue to haunt you years from now. Nothing is ever truly deleted in cyber-space but can remain accessible forever.

Sex and Technology

It's natural for teenagers to have strong sexual desires, and in this day and age, it's common for them to use technology to satisfy them. They might believe that there's no real risk to sexting or cybersex—the sending of sexually explicit messages or photographs to another boy or girl via text messages and instant messages. However, if teens aren't careful, they can get into serious trouble.

When you participate in sexting or cybersex, you create text and picture files that last forever. And they can spread. In one instance in New Hartford, New York, a boy sent a revealing photo of himself to a girl. She for-warded the picture to some friends, who forwarded it to more friends. By the time school officials discovered the photo, about three hundred students had seen it.

Needless to say, you'd be embarrassed if your nude photos spread, but there are even more serious conse-quences than humiliation. Your photos can be used to blackmail you. In other words, a person could threaten to make your photos public unless you do what he or she says.

If you send explicit photos of yourself or another class-mate, you can even go to jail. It doesn't matter how old you are or if you only send photos of yourself. It's illegal to create, possess, or distribute explicit images of a minor. You can be arrested for breaking child pornography laws. If you don't go to jail, you may still have to register as a

A sexual text or photo that you send to just one friend may quickly be forwarded to hundreds of classmates and strangers. Even your family members may see it.

sex offender for the rest of your life. And any potential employers would be made aware of your status as a convicted and registered sex offender.

If you receive an explicit photo of a classmate, do not forward it to anyone. Tell a teacher immediately. Though that classmate may be punished, teachers and school administrators could stop the photograph's circulation and prevent even worse consequences.

There's nothing wrong with having sexual feelings, but it's important to use your head. Otherwise, you could suffer a lifetime of consequences for a few brief moments of enjoyment or a cheap thrill.

The Opposite Sex

You interact with women every day in many different capacities. A lot of these women serve important roles in your life, like your mother, a teacher, a boss in an after-school job, a friend, a sister, an aunt, or a grandmother. As you grow up, you will work with women and you might marry one. You may even have a daughter someday. You will always be a part of a complex and vital web of female relationships. For this reason, you need to treat women respectfully or else risk missing out on some of the most valuable and rewarding relationships in your life.

Boys and girls are much more alike than we realize. Still, we consider them to be completely different. We even refer to each other as "the opposite sex," as if we're completely different from each other in every single respect, large and small. This type of thinking can make it difficult for us to relate to girls. While it's true that boys and girls

Forming a friendship with a girl can be an enormously enriching experience, one that allows you greater opportunity to explore and express your emotions and gain a different perspective on things.

are typically different, it's only because they're taught to be different; they are not born that way. We should instead focus on our many similarities. It's important to remember that we're all human beings, whether male or female, and we all deserve equal treatment.

There are many advantages to being friends with a girl. Since they have different experiences, girls tend to have a different outlook on life than boys do. That additional perspective may help boys solve problems they wouldn't be able to otherwise. Also, it might be easier to discuss your feelings with a girl than with another guy. You may

worry that a guy friend will make fun of you, but girls are usually more comfortable discussing emotions. They can help you identify your feelings and figure out how to handle them. Overall, it can be easier to show girls your gentler, more sensitive side. In fact, most girls value those qualities that boys usually make fun of, like kindness, openness, and warmth.

Of course, all girls are not the same. Every relationship is different from person to person. You may even be fine discussing your emotions with a guy. However, you might find that a female friend can fill a role that your guy friends can't. Either way, it's important to be close with girls so that you're able to interact with the "not-so-opposite" sex.

Becoming Men

Every day, we feel pressure to "act like men." We try to prove our manhood to others by copying masculine stereotypes. We may even succeed. Yet even when we feel we've proven our manhood in a specific instance, it's always only temporary. As soon as we inevitably demonstrate less masculine traits, our manhood will be questioned once again. We'll have to prove our masculinity over and over, again and again, for the rest of our lives.

Don't worry, though, because it doesn't matter. You don't actually have to prove your masculinity to anyone. You can be macho or not. Either way, you will become a man, and nothing anyone says can change that. We try to behave like we're expected to because it always seems easier to fit in that way, but it never actually is. Conforming to some ideal that doesn't suit who you really are is hard—maybe even impossible—work. It requires ignoring your self, and it's impossible to be happy that way. Now that you know, it's up to you whether or not you'll let other people's unrealistic concepts of masculinity pressure you.

You don't have to focus on becoming a man. That happens automatically and inevitably throughout puberty and adolescence. What you should focus on is what type of man you are becoming and will become. The world has more than enough macho men, but never enough good men. Live up to your own values. Be yourself. Love yourself. The rest will follow.

Ten Great Questions
to Ask a Guidance Counselor

1.
What is the difference between bullying and sexual harassment?

2.
How do you know the difference between "joking around" and bullying?

3.
What do I do if someone is bullying me online?

4.
What do I do if someone is spreading rumors about me?

5.
My friend is trying to pressure me into doing something I don't want to do. How can I resist?

6.
How do I tell my friend that I'm angry with him or her?

7.
Why does it seem hard for boys and girls to be friends?

8.
My boyfriend or girlfriend wants to have sex, but I'm not ready. What can I do?

9.
What do I do if someone puts an embarrassing photo of me on a social networking Web site?

10.
A friend sent me an explicit photo of another classmate. What should I do?

body image A person's concept of the attractiveness of his or her own physical appearance, usually in relation to some sort of "ideal."

cyberbullying The use of any digital communication technology, like a cell phone or the Internet, to bully, threaten, humiliate, intimidate, or otherwise harm another person.

double standard Any set of principles containing different provisions for one group of people than for another.

gender A set of social characteristics that display or demonstrate an individual's sex to others.

gender roles Set of social behaviors, interests, and activities that are widely considered to be socially appropriate for individuals of a specific sex.

GLBT Gay, lesbian, bisexual, and transgender.

homophobia Unreasonable fear or hatred of homosexuality and homosexuals.

homosexuality Sexual desires or behavior directed toward persons of one's own sex.

masculinity The basic characteristics of manliness, as defined by one's society and culture.

mass media All media technologies used for communication with a vast audience, such as television, movies, the Internet, newspapers, magazines, advertising, radio, and music, and the organizations that control them.

nature vs. nurture A debate over the relative importance of the qualities an individual is born with ("nature") versus his or her personal experience and environment ("nurture") in determining individual differences.

objectify To present and conceive of a human being as a mere object, without a will, a personality, a self, or any inner life, to be used and consumed by the viewer.

peer pressure A persuasive force exerted on someone by his or her friends or acquaintances to do something he or she doesn't really want to do.

sex Biological characteristics that determine if a person is male or female.

sexual harassment Intimidation, coercion, or bullying of a sexual nature.

sexual identity How a person describes or characterizes his or her sexuality to others.

sexuality The way someone expresses awareness of his or her biological sex and capacity for sexual feelings.

sexual orientation A pattern of emotional, romantic, or sexual attraction to men, women, both genders, or neither genders.

stereotype A popular belief about specific types of individuals based on some prior and very narrow assumptions.

transgender General term applied to a variety of individuals, behaviors, and groups involving tendencies to vary from the usual gender roles. The term can encompass individuals living and dressing as members of the opposite sex or physically and chemically altering their body to actually change their gender.

Gay-Straight Alliance Network
1550 Bryant Street, Suite 800
San Francisco, CA 94103
(415) 552-4229
Web site: http://www.gsanetwork.org
Organization that supports youth gay-straight alliances.

Lesbian Gay Bi Trans Youth Line
P.O. Box 62, Station "F"
Toronto, ON M4Y 2L4
Canada
(800) 268-9688
Web site: http://www.youthline.ca
Service that provides support, information, and referrals to
    GLBT teens.

Media Awareness Network (MNet)
950 Gladstone Avenue, Suite 120
Ottawa, ON K1Y 3E6
Canada
(613) 224-7721
Toll Free: (800) 896-3342 (in Canada)
Web site: http://www.media-awareness.ca/english/
    index.cfm
MNet is a Canadian nonprofit organization that has been
    pioneering the development of media literacy and
    digital literacy programs since its incorporation in

1996. It is home to one of the world's most compre-
hensive collections of media literacy and digital
literacy resources. MNet focuses its efforts on developing the information and tools necessary to help young
people understand how the media works, how the
media may affect their lifestyle choices, and the extent
to which they, as consumers and citizens, are being
well informed.

MyGSA.ca
185 Carlton Street
Toronto, ON M5A 2K7
(888) 204-7777
Web site: http://mygsa.ca
An organization providing a safe place online to form a
    GLBT teen community .

National Youth Leadership Council (NYLC)
1667 Snelling Avenue North
St. Paul, MN 55108
(651) 631-3672
Web site: http://www.nylc.org
The NYLC is devoted to helping young people become
    leaders via community involvement.

Parents, Families, and Friends of Lesbians & Gays (PFLAG)
1828 L Street NW
Suite 660
Washington, D.C. 20036
(202) 467-8180

Web site: http://www.pflag.org
Via support, education, and advocacy, PFLAG promotes
   the well-being and health of gay, lesbian, bisexual, and
   transgendered people, as well as their family and
   friends.

Planned Parenthood Federation of America
434 West 33rd Street
New York, NY 10001
(212) 541-7800
Web site: http://www.plannedparenthood.org
Planned Parenthood provides sexual health information and
   health care services.

Students Against Destructive Decisions (SADD)
P.O. Box 800
Marlboro, MA 01752
(877) SADD-INC (723-3462)
Web site: http://www.saddonline.com
SADD is a student-based organization that was originally
   founded to combat underage drinking and drunk
   driving. Since then, it has expanded its mission to
   address issues such as drug abuse, violence, STDs,
   and suicide.

The Trevor Project
Administrative Offices
8704 Santa Monica Boulevard, Suite 200
West Hollywood, CA 90069

(310) 271-8845

Web site: http://www.thetrevorproject.org

An organization that provides life-affirming support for
   GLBT teens.

Web Sites

Due to the changing nature of Internet links, Rosen
Publishing has developed an online list of Web sites
related to the subject of this book. This site is updated
regularly. Please use this link to access this list:

http://www.rosenlinks.com/ymg/ssid

Alsenas, Linas. *Gay America: Struggle for Equality*. New York, NY: Amulet Books, 2008.

Beckman, Wendy Hart. *Dating, Relationships, and Sexuality: What Teens Should Know*. Berkeley Heights, NJ: Enslow Publishers, 2006.

Boyett, Jason. *A Guy's Guide to Life: How to Become a Man in 224 Pages or Less*. Nashville, TN: Thomas Nelson, 2010.

Corinna, Heather. *S.E.X.: The All-You-Need-to-Know Progressive Sexuality Guide to Get You Through High School and College*. Cambridge, MA: Da Capo Press, 2007.

Covey, Sean. *The 6 Most Important Decisions You'll Ever Make: A Guide for Teens*. New York, NY: Fireside, 2006.

Eaklor, Vicki L. *Queer America: A GLBT History of the 20th Century*. Santa Barbara, CA: Greenwood, 2008.

Garden, Nancy. *Hear Us Out!: Lesbian and Gay Stories of Struggle, Progress, and Hope, 1950 to the Present*. New York, NY: Farrar, Straus and Giroux, 2007.

Gideonse, Ted. *From Boys to Men: Gay Men Write About Growing Up*. Cambridge, MA: Da Capo Press, 2006.

Jacobs, Thomas A. *Teen Cyberbullying Investigated: Where Do Your Rights End and Consequences Begin?* Minneapolis, MN: Free Spirit Publishing, 2010.

Koertge, Ron. *Boy Girl Boy*. New York, NY: Graphia, 2007.

Kuhn, Betsy. *Gay Power!: The Stonewall Riots and the Gay Rights Movement, 1969* (Civil Rights Struggles Around the World). Minneapolis, MN: Twenty-First Century Books, 2011.

Marcus, Eric. *What If Someone I Know Is Gay?: Answers to Questions About What It Means to Be Gay and Lesbian.* New York, NY: Simon Pulse, 2007.

Miller, Karen. *Male and Female Roles* (Opposing Viewpoints). Farmington Hills, MI: Greenhaven, 2009.

Payment, Simone. *Friendship, Dating, and Relationships* (Teens: Being Gay, Lesbian, Bisexual, or Transgender). New York, NY: Rosen Publishing, 2010.

Rivero, Lisa. *Smart Teens' Guide to Living with Intensity: How to Get More Out of Life and Learning.* Scottsdale, AZ: Great Potential Press, 2010.

Simmons, Danette. *Teen Reflections: My Life, My Journey, My Story.* Charleston, SC: CreateSpace, 2010.

Tompkins, Michael A., and Katherine A. Martinez. *My Anxious Mind: A Teen's Guide to Managing Anxiety and Panic.* Washington, DC: Magination Press, 2009.

Wadham, Rachel L. *This Is My Life: A Guide to Realistic Fiction for Teens* (Genreflecting Advisory Series). Santa Barbara, CA: Libraries Unlimited, 2010.

BIBLIOGRAPHY

American Academy of Child & Adolescent Psychiatry. "Bullying." May 2008. Retrieved January 2011 (http://aacap.org/page.ww?name=Bullying&section= Facts+for+Families).

Bateman, Geoffrey W. "AIDS Activism." GLBTQ.com. Retrieved January 2011 (http://www.glbtq.com/ social-sciences/aids_activism.html).

Bilton, Nick. "Burglars Said to Have Picked Houses Based on Facebook Updates." *New York Times*, September 12, 2010. Retrieved January 2011 (http://bits.blogs. nytimes.com/2010/09/12/burglars-picked-houses- based-on-facebook-updates/).

Cromie, William J. "Male Body Image: East Doesn't Meet West." *Harvard University Gazette*, February 10, 2005. Retrieved January 2011 (http://www.news.harvard. edu/gazette/2005/02.10/11-bodyimage.html).

Ebert, Roger. "Movie Answer Man." RogerEbert.com, November 16, 2003. Retrieved January 2011 (http://rogerebert.suntimes.com/apps/pbcs.dll/ article?AID=/20031116/ANSWERMAN/ 311160302).

Elish, Jill. "FSU Study Finds Body Image Stereotypes May Begin in the High Chair." *Florida State University News*, December 15, 2005. Retrieved January 2011 (http://www.fsu.edu/news/2005/12/15/ body.image/).

FCC.gov. "Obscene, Indecent, and Profane Broadcasts."
Retrieved January 2011 (http://www.fcc.gov/cgb/
consumerfacts/obscene.html).

Grabmeier, Jeff. "Domestic Violence Often Comes from
Men Who Repress Emotions, Feel Threatened, Study
Finds." Ohio State University Research Online,
December 9, 2002. Retrieved January 2011 (http://
researchnews.osu.edu/archive/violstres.htm).

Kimmel, Michael S. Manhood in America: A Cultural History.
2nd Ed. New York, NY: Oxford University Press, 2006.

Lenhart, Amanda. "Cyberbullying." Pew Internet, June 27,
2007. Retrieved January 2011 (http://pewinternet.
org/Reports/2007/Cyberbullying/1-Findings.aspx).

Liebowitz, Matt. "Facebook Used to Get to Nude E-mail
Photos." MSNBC.com, January 14, 2010. Retrieved
January 2011 (http://www.msnbc.msn.com/
id/41082627/ns/technology_and_science-security/).

Lorber, Judith, "'Night to His Day': The Social Construction
of Gender." The Spirit of Sociology: A Reader. Ron
Matson, ed. Upper Saddle River, NJ: Pearson
Education, Inc., 2005, pp. 292–305.

McKie, Robin. "Male and Female Ability Differences Down
to Socialization, Not Genetics." The Observer Online,
August 15, 2010. Retrieved January 2011 (http://
www.guardian.co.uk/world/2010/aug/15/
girls-boys-think-same-way).

NYTimes.com. "Adolescent Depression." Retrieved January
2011 (http://health.nytimes.com/health/guides/
disease/adolescent-depression/overview.html).

NYTimes.com. "Stonewall Rebellion." April 10, 2009. Retrieved January 2011 (http://topics.nytimes.com/topics/reference/timestopics/subjects/s/stonewall_rebellion/index.htm).

PBS Parents. "Boys in School." Retrieved January 2011 (http://www.pbs.org/parents/raisingboys/school.html).

Savin-Williams, Ritch C. "...And Then I Became Gay": Young Men's Stories. London, England: Routledge, 1998.

Shaffer, Susan Morris, and Linda Perlman Gordon. Why Boy's Don't Talk and Why It Matters: A Parent's Survival Guide to Connecting with Your Teen. New York, NY: McGraw Hill, 2005.

Shepherd, Jessica, and Sue Learner. "Lessons on Gay History Cut Homophobic Bullying in North London School." Guardian.co.uk, October 26, 2010. Retrieved January 2011 (http://www.guardian.co.uk/education/2010/oct/26/gay-history-lessons-bullying-schools).

Silverstein, Olga, and Beth Rashbaum. The Courage to Raise Good Men. New York, NY: Penguin, 1995.

Stanford University Encyclopedia of Philosophy. "Homosexuality." August 6, 2002. Retrieved January 2011 (http://plato.stanford.edu/entries/homosexuality/).

S

T

U

W

X

About the Author

Joe Craig is an author who is dedicated to promoting individuality, creativity, and self-confidence in teenagers. Like most men, he's familiar with the pressures of living up to the masculine "ideal." He has two younger brothers. In his free time, he enjoys watching football and painting.

Photo Credits

Cover, back cover, chapter openers, pp. 19, 29, 52–53, 76–77, 86–87 Shutterstock; pp. 6–7 Rubberball/Mike Kemp/Getty Images; pp. 10–11 Lou Jones/The Image Bank/Getty Images; pp. 12–13 Tony Anderson/Taxi/Getty Images; p. 17 Al Messerschmidt/Getty Images Sport/Getty Images; pp. 26–27, 68–69 Image Source/Image Source Getty Images; pp. 30–31 Mike Powell/Lifesize/Getty Images; p. 36 Kevork Djansezian/Getty Images Sport/Getty Images; pp. 40–41 Hemera/Thinkstock; pp. 42–43 Jack Slomovits/Photodisc/Getty Images; pp. 44–45 JGI/Tom Grill/Blend Images/Getty Images; pp. 48–49 Jupiterimages/ Creatas/Thinkstock; pp. 56–57 © www.istockphoto.com/ Harry Lines; pp. 60–61 New York Daily News Archives/ New York Daily News via Getty Images; pp. 62–63 Doug Menuez/Photodisc/Getty Images; pp. 64–65, 70–71 SW Productions/Photodisc/Getty Images; pp. 74–75 Banana Stock/Banana Stock/Thinkstock; p. 80 Hemara/Getty Images; p. 84 Jupiterimages/Pixland/Getty Images.

Designer

Designer: Nicole Russo; Photo Researcher: Marty Levick